Beat procrastination and distraction

The Easy ways to beat procrastinating,
Master Your Time and Boost Productivity.

William Spann

Table of content

Procrastination is the enemy of success

If you are a normal human being, then you will not be immune to the temptation of "putting off till tomorrow that which should be done today."

Despite all our best intentions to be efficient and successful, the tendency of putting work aside till the last minute is all too strong. Important components of our professional, scholastic, and even personal life are frequently not done properly, since we succumb to the "it can wait another day" mindset.

Procrastination is the enemy of our success on several fronts. Waiting till the latest available minute to handle an essential duty will more often than not result in lowered potential and performance, and in extreme situations might cause failure.

Putting off a job report, or an academic article, or even neglecting to manage your personal life in a timely way may affect your intended results and make you look unprofessional, sloppy, or careless. To be honest and to the point, the proverb "you can either pay now or pay later" is embodied when you make the purposeful choice to cave to your lethargy.

Procrastination is a normal habit that many individuals fight daily. It is the act of delaying duties or activities that we know should be completed in favor of something more fun or easy. While it may appear innocuous in the near term, procrastination may have major effects in the long run. It may not only inhibit personal development and accomplishment, but it can also contribute to increased worry and anxiety.

One of the key ways in which procrastination is the enemy of success is that it inhibits you from taking action. Success involves hard effort, commitment, and action. When we delay, we are not putting forth the required effort to attain our objectives. You are putting off what has to be done in favor of more fun or simpler chores. This lack of action may lead to lost chances and a lack of development.

Procrastination may also contribute to lower productivity. When you put off chores till the last minute, you are generally harried and stressed. This might lead to mediocre work since we are not able to offer your whole concentration and effort to the job at hand. This may be particularly detrimental in academic and professional environments, where high-quality work is required.

Not only can procrastination delay you from accomplishing your objectives, but it may also have detrimental repercussions on your mental health. The more you put off things, the more nervous and agitated you may get. This is because you are aware of the tasks that we are not competing with, and we are constantly thinking about them. This might lead to emotions of guilt and shame, which can further influence your drive and productivity.

Overall, procrastination is a major enemy of success. It prevents you from taking action, leads to decreased productivity, and can have negative effects on our mental health. To fight procrastination, it is vital to establish clear objectives, make a routine, and keep ourselves responsible. With dedication and effort, you can overcome procrastination and achieve our desired level of success.

What causes extreme procrastination

Extreme procrastination, or chronic procrastination, may be induced by a multitude of circumstances. Some common reasons include:

Perfectionism: Some individuals may have unreasonable expectations of themselves and worry that they will not be able to finish work to their high standards. This might lead to procrastination as they strive to avoid the prospect of failure or disappointment.

Lack of motivation or interest: If a job is not personally meaningful or pleasurable, it may be difficult to find the drive to accomplish it.

Difficulty with time management: Some individuals may struggle with planning and managing their time properly, resulting in procrastination as they strive to accomplish chores at the last minute.

Difficulty with task initiation: Some individuals may have problems getting started on a task, even if they are motivated and engaged in it. This might be due to a lack of attention or a propensity to get easily distracted.

Stress and anxiety: Procrastination may sometimes be a technique for dealing with stress or worry since it helps individuals to escape the discomfort or pressure connected with a tough activity.

Fear of success or failure: Some individuals may delay because they are terrified of achieving and the possible duties or expectations that may come with it, or because they are afraid of failing and the potential repercussions.

Procrastinating as a coping mechanism: In certain situations, procrastination may be a means of dealing with underlying difficulties such as depression, poor self-esteem, or other mental health challenges.

How procrastination affect mental health

Procrastination is the act of delaying or postponing tasks or decisions. While it may seem like a harmless habit, it can have negative impacts on an individual's mental health.

One way that procrastination can affect mental health is through increased stress and anxiety. When we put off tasks, they often pile up and become overwhelming. This can lead to feelings of anxiety and stress as we struggle to catch up and meet deadlines.

Procrastination can also lead to feelings of guilt and shame. When we put off tasks or avoid making decisions, we may feel like we are letting ourselves and others down. This can lead to low self-esteem and negative self-perception.

Procrastination can also contribute to feelings of depression. When we constantly avoid tasks or fail to meet deadlines, we may feel a sense of hopelessness and failure. This can lead to feelings of despair and a lack of motivation to engage in activities.

In addition to these negative mental health impacts, procrastination can also lead to physical health problems. For example, if we are constantly stressed and anxious due to procrastination, it can lead to issues such as insomnia, stomach problems, and an increased risk of heart disease.

Overall, procrastination can have significant negative impacts on mental health. It is important to address and overcome this habit to improve overall well-being. Some ways for combating procrastination include defining clear objectives, splitting things into smaller portions, and getting assistance from friends or a therapist.

Beating procrastination in the digital age

Procrastination is a frequent issue that may impede individuals from accomplishing their objectives and finishing critical activities. In the digital era, it may be particularly simple to be sidetracked by the myriad of diversions and distractions accessible online. However, various ways might help you combat procrastination and remain focused on your task.

Identify the core reason for your procrastination: It's crucial to understand why you are delaying successfully solving the issue. Some typical reasons for procrastination include a lack of desire, unclear objectives, trouble getting started, and a lack of structure.

Set clear and detailed goals: Having a clear grasp of what you want to achieve might help you remain motivated and focused on your job. Make sure your objectives are detailed and quantifiable and consider creating deadlines to help you remain on track.

Create a to-do list: A to-do list may help you organize your chores and prioritize the most critical ones. Break major jobs into smaller, more manageable portions, and check off things as you do them to help you experience a feeling of success.

Eliminate distractions: It might be tough to keep concentrated when you have too many distractions around you. Consider turning off alerts on your phone or computer, or finding a quiet spot to work where you won't be distracted.

Use a time management technique: Various time management approaches may help you keep organized and focused on your job. One common strategy is the Pomodoro Technique, which entails working for a specific length of time (typically 25 minutes) and then taking a brief break (usually 5 minutes) (usually 5 minutes).

Find accountability: It might be beneficial to have someone to keep you responsible for your progress. Consider engaging with a mentor or coach, or finding an accountability partner who can help you remain on track.

Take care of yourself: It's crucial to take care of your physical and mental health to be focused and productive. Make sure you get adequate sleep, exercise frequently, and take pauses to relax and rejuvenate.

By applying these tactics, you may conquer procrastination and be more productive in the digital era.

Distractions that causes procrastination

Ever sat at your work and wondered why you procrastinate? Then, just when you may be getting to the bottom of your thought process, you realize that thinking about procrastination is one of the reasons why you aren't getting any work done.

The secret to productivity is to spend your time dancing around distractions that are continuously thrown your way. One interruption, even the smallest disturbance, may be enough to send you down a procrastination vortex of no return.
To avoid these distractions, you must be aware of them. Here are six activities we do each day that are distracting.

1. Incoming emails
When was the last time you checked your emails?

We check our emails way too often because we've created this myth that every email needs to be responded to immediately. This, of course, isn't true. If something were truly that important, then we'd get a phone call instead of a message in our inbox.

Emails can wait. They are distractions that will always be there for you when we don't want to focus on our work. Yes, they're very dependable when we want to think about anything other than the task at hand.

Check emails less. Set a time at the end of the day to look through your email. But whatever you do, don't check them before that time.

2. Overheard phone talks

Have you ever discovered a peaceful spot to work, then all of a sudden someone sits down right next to you and begins chatting on the phone?

No big thing, right? You can ignore them and continue to concentrate on your task.

Wrong.

It turns out that overhearing one-sided phone conversations distracts 82% of individuals. Not knowing how the person you're listening to will answer is more compelling and makes you want to pay attention.

This might be irritating since you find a great calm area, and you don't want to give it up. But, if someone is on the phone then you should choose another spot that makes it simpler for you to concentrate.

3. Social media

Just one minute. That's all you said. I'll check Facebook for a minute. How has an hour gone by?

Social media is the greatest distractor of all. It's a constant stream of fresh stuff that never ceases. It doesn't matter when you click on Facebook or peruse through Twitter.

There's always something fresh that takes you away from your job.

I realize this isn't an easy thing to avoid. After all, social media is incredibly addictive. But you have to try. Put your phone in airplane mode. Turn it off altogether. Put it in the break room if you have to. Download software that makes it hard for you to access your social network accounts.

This is a distraction you're going to want to go the additional mile to eradicate.

4. Listening to music

You're meant to put on headphones, play your favorite songs, and block out the loud workplace. Right?

Not exactly. Music might be distracting if you're undertaking cognitively demanding activities.

Are you working on anything that needs critical thinking? Are you attempting to solve an issue or find out the best method to achieve something? Then music is most likely distracting you and making it more difficult for you to accomplish your activity. Throw the headphones beneath your desk and start thinking.

5. Always saying yes

Right now you should be concentrating on reducing distractions. However, it's conceivable that you're merely generating additional distractions for yourself.

Learn to say no. Meetings, chores, and favors aren't always useful to your productivity. Instead, they're merely distractions that are blocking you from focusing on the vital task.

Make sure you properly assess each offer that comes your way. If it doesn't help you reach your objective or complete the job you should be working on, then it's better if you turn it down. Giving yourself extra obligations would simply pull you away from the job that counts the most.

6. New ideas

You're attempting to work on an assignment that's due at the end of the day. When, suddenly, you have an idea for something spectacular! This notion frantically captures your attention and clings it hard.

Don't allow it.

This phenomenon is known as idea hopping, which is when your creativity kicks in and starts coming up with new ideas while you're already working on something. This happens because you want to distract yourself so badly that you're willing to think of something entirely new to convince yourself you aren't spending your time wisely.

Take out a piece of paper. Write down the idea so you can go back to it later. Then forget about it. You have a task you have to complete and now is not the time to start something entirely new.

It's Up to You
The distractions that are consuming your work life are most likely caused by you. Do all you can to get rid of these distractions and concentrate on your task. You will rapidly realize how overcoming procrastination can favorably affect your life.

what causes distraction

Distraction is a bane of contemporary life. Between our mobile phones and computer displays, not to mention our kids and colleagues, our attention is always being distracted. It might become difficult to concentrate on any one task—or any one person—for very long.

If anything, the world is becoming a more distracting place. Technology is getting increasingly widespread and persuasive. But hope tech businesses improve their practices and your employer eventually learns to respect your time may take longer than you're ready to wait. Better to prepare yourself to control distraction with tactics you can adopt right now. After all, while distractions aren't always your fault, handling them is your obligation.

Distraction is created by items that pull our attention away from the work at hand.

These distractions might originate from external sources, such as noise or other people, or internal causes, such as our thoughts or feelings. Some typical reasons for distraction include:

Noise or other external distractions: These might include loud sounds, music, or people conversing nearby.

Internal distractions: These might include our thoughts, emotions, or bodily feelings, such as hunger or pain.

Multitasking: When we attempt to perform more than one item at a time, it may be difficult to completely concentrate on any one job, resulting in distraction.

Boredom: When we are not engaged in the activity at hand, it might be difficult to remain concentrated, leading to distraction.

Lack of motivation: When we are not driven to accomplish a job, it may be challenging to remain concentrated and prevent distraction.

Information overload: When we are provided with too much information at once, it might be difficult to comprehend it all and remain focused on the work at hand.

Stress or anxiety: These feelings may make it difficult to concentrate and remain focused, resulting in distraction.

dealing with digital distraction

Do you regularly check your phone during class, work, or social settings? When you are taking a class online from home, are you interrupted or distracted by alerts or the temptation to check for them? Do you stop studying every few minutes to text, check your social media, or watch a YouTube video? If this is you, realize that you are not alone. While digital distractions are not uncommon, they may be destructive to your study habits, interrupting your attention and turning your reading or studying habits unproductive.

The good news is that there are ways that may help you overcome harmful technological habits and recenter your attention on your schoolwork. This handout includes suggestions and resources to help you eliminate distractions and remain on track when it counts most

Digital distractions may be a huge difficulty in today's society, as we are continuously inundated with messages and alerts from our gadgets. Here are a few ideas for coping with internet distractions:

Set boundaries: Consider defining defined times when you will not check your phone or other gadgets. For example, you may decide not to glance at your phone after a specific hour in the evening or not to check it first thing in the morning.

Turn off notifications: Consider turning off notifications for applications that are not needed or that you find especially bothersome. You may also personalize your alerts so that you only get them for the most essential messages.

Use applications to assist manage your time: There are several tools available that can help you remain focused and manage your time more successfully. These programs may block distracting websites, impose limitations on your device use, or give reminders to take breaks.

Take breaks: It's crucial to take breaks from your gadgets and spend time away from displays. This might help you refresh and remain focused when you do need to work on your computer or phone.

Find other methods to relax: Instead of leaning on your electronics for relaxation or amusement, try finding other ways to decompress. This might include hobbies such as reading, jogging, or spending time with friends and family.

dealing with distraction in business

As you sit down to read this book, I'm sure you've faced distractions at work at least once today, maybe more than once.

Chances are you may get interrupted before you finish reading this book.

The basic reality is that we all confront distractions at work every single day, and generally every single hour, something or someone may lead you to be sidetracked.

With so many meetings to attend, talks or drop-ins by colleagues, calls, emails, social alerts, and countless more distractions, it may sometimes seem like a real effort to be productive and get the vital things done.

Distractions diminish our productivity and vitality.

They impact our capacity to concentrate and persist with projects or activities long enough to see them through.

If you think about your working week, I'm sure you can list down 5 to 10 items or persons who have produced distractions at work.

But how many of those distractions are self-inflicted and how many are the product of your working environment?

Distractions may be a huge obstacle to productivity and success in business. Here are some ways that might help you cope with distractions and remain focused:

Identify the sources of distraction: The first step is to identify the sources of distraction that are harming your productivity. These might be external distractions such as noise or interruptions, or interior distractions such as your thoughts or feelings.

Set limits: Set boundaries around when and how you will be accessible to others. This can mean locking your office door, placing a "do not disturb" sign, or defining particular hours for checking emails.

Use tools to prevent distractions: Some several products and applications can help you block distractions, such as website blockers or noise-canceling headphones.

Create a pleasant work environment: A comfortable and orderly workspace may assist eliminate distractions and enhance productivity.

Take pauses: It's crucial to take breaks and give your mind a chance to recover. This may help you remain focused and prevent burnout.

Practice mindfulness: Mindfulness is the practice of paying attention to the present moment. By being mindful, you can train your brain to stay focused on the task at hand and not get easily distracted.

Set specific goals and deadlines: Having clear goals and deadlines can help you stay focused and motivated.

By following these strategies, you can effectively manage distractions and stay focused on your work.

dealing with distractions at work

It might be tough to keep concentrated in a hectic workplace. There are phone calls to take and emails to answer – not to mention the appeal of a fast text or Snapchat to your buddies.

Small distractions might seem quite innocuous (after all, what's two minutes out of an eight-hour day?) Yet frequent interruptions may wreak havoc on your productivity, and severely damage the quality of your work.

Tweet me!

If you find yourself being easily distracted by colleagues? discussions, people passing by your desk, or email notifications flashing up on your computer, check out our top five strategies to help you limit interruptions and enhance your attention.

Work beside productive individuals. Focus may be infectious, so if feasible, surround yourself with the most productive individuals in the company. Sitting next to or working with someone who knuckles down can not only motivate you to do the same but also minimize your probability of getting interrupted needlessly.

Break tasks into parts. Large jobs might appear daunting, which can drive us to welcome interruptions, and lower our productivity. If you divide a job up into smaller activities that demand less time, you'll feel like the overall objective is more feasible. Smaller activities are often simpler to do – guaranteeing you're more likely to remain concentrated on having each mini-task accomplished.

Set limits with interrupting coworkers. If you work with someone prone to distraction, consider creating some limits so they know when you need to focus on the job at hand. You may tell someone you need to work on a certain assignment respectfully without hurting their emotions. Let them know you'll be with them in just a few minutes to address their question.

Block online distractions. If you find it impossible to ignore social media or your favorite blog, try buying one of the distraction-free applications available, such as Anti-Social or Concentrate. These will ban you from selected sites for designated periods.

Make time for breaks. It may seem paradoxical to recommend frequent pauses, but they are necessary to give your brain a rest, incorporate social time in the day, and re-energize and motivate yourself for the next job on your list.

How to focus and ignore distraction

Learning how to not become sidetracked is a challenging objective to have. Most days, you sit at your desk, eager to finally get some work done. "Okay, let's do this," you think to yourself. You navigate over to Word or Google Drive and start up a new document. You have some sense of what has to be done, but what occurs next?

You scribble a few words down but simply can't remain focused. Then you say, "Maybe I should wake myself up with something fun." You go to Facebook, and 20 minutes are gone. Then follows an hour of idly viewing a handful of YouTube videos. Before you know it, noon has arrived, and half the day is gone.

If you're a normal working American, you'll be distracted every 11 minutes; and, it will take you 25 minutes to settle down again to your job.

Additionally, the more intricate your project, the longer it will take to restore your attention. This arises because your brain needs to put forth tremendous effort while moving between difficult tasks.

Distractions have a big impact on our attention and productivity. There are various ways that you may use to help you concentrate and avoid distractions:

Find a quiet, dedicated workspace: Look for a spot where you can reduce interruptions and concentrate on your job. This might be a peaceful area in your house, a coffee shop, or a coworking place.

Set particular times for work and breaks: Use a timer or timetable to help you remain on track. Plan to work for a specified length of time, and then take a brief break to relax and refuel.

Develop a to-do list: Prioritize your tasks and create a list that helps you keep focused on what has to be done. This may help you keep on track and prevent feeling overwhelmed.

Switch off notifications: If feasible, turn off notifications on your phone or computer to prevent being continuously disturbed by alerts.

Use tools to block distracting websites: There are applications and apps available that can block distracting websites or restrict your access to them during particular periods of the day.

Take breaks: It's crucial to take pauses to relax and rejuvenate. During your breaks, do something that helps you relax and clear your thoughts, such as going for a walk, meditating, or practicing a hobby.

Practice mindfulness: Pay attention to your thoughts and concentrate on the current moment. This might help you remain grounded and avoid getting caught up in diversions.

Get adequate sleep: Make sure you're getting enough sleep at night to help you feel more awake and focused throughout the day.

Exercise regularly: Exercise may enhance your physical and mental well-being, which can help you concentrate and remain motivated.

Easy ways to stop procrastinating and getting distracted

As I sit here writing this piece, I just have my laptop and water bottle in front of me, I'm listening to some concentrated music with my noise-canceling headphones, all of the alerts on my phone and laptop are off and the only open internet tab is the Google Doc that I'm working on. This is my hyperfocus setup. This is how I'm at my most productive. This is how I can perform distraction-free, intense work.

Do you know why this works so well?
Because my brain has nothing else to pay attention to. All of the things that are more new and enjoyable are pulled out of my

surroundings during these heavy work hours. In other words, there is nothing else to do but write.

And when your job becomes the most interesting alternative there is for your brain (since there is nothing else accessible) you'll start to put all of your mental resources to use on your task. Goodbye, procrastinating! Here are some ways that may help you quit procrastinating and remain focused on tasks:

Set defined and attainable objectives: Having clear and specific goals will help you keep motivated and on track. Break major objectives into smaller, more achievable activities and concentrate on finishing one job at a time.

Create a schedule: Scheduling your time might help you remain organized and prioritize your responsibilities. Set up allocated blocks of time for certain chores and attempt to keep to your plan as precisely as possible.

Remove distractions: Identify the things that distract you and strive to eliminate or reduce them as much as possible. This may entail eliminating unneeded tabs on your computer, silencing your phone, or finding a quiet spot to work.

Take breaks: It's crucial to take pauses to refresh and concentrate. Step away from your job for a few minutes every hour or so to stretch, take a stroll, or do anything else that helps you relax.

Use productivity tools: There are various tools and applications available that may help you keep focused and on track. For example, you may use a timer to split your work into small pieces and take breaks in between, or use a to-do list app to keep track of your activities and progress.

Seek accountability: Consider finding someone to keep you responsible for your objectives and activities. This might be a friend, family member, or professional coach. Having someone to check in with might help you keep motivated and on track.

Printed in Great Britain
by Amazon